MAR   2015

ARIZONA CARDINALS

THE STORY OF THE

NFL TODAY

THE STORY OF THE ARIZONA CARDINALS

JIM WHITING

CREATIVE EDUCATION

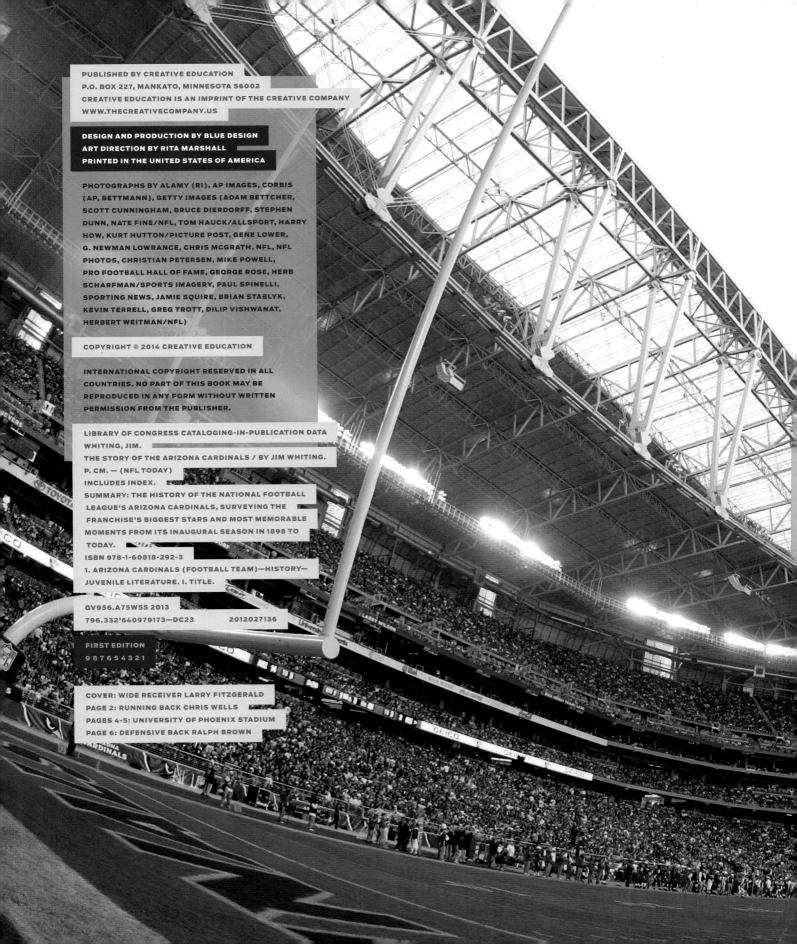

PUBLISHED BY CREATIVE EDUCATION
P.O. BOX 227, MANKATO, MINNESOTA 56002
CREATIVE EDUCATION IS AN IMPRINT OF THE CREATIVE COMPANY
WWW.THECREATIVECOMPANY.US

DESIGN AND PRODUCTION BY BLUE DESIGN
ART DIRECTION BY RITA MARSHALL
PRINTED IN THE UNITED STATES OF AMERICA

PHOTOGRAPHS BY ALAMY (RI), AP IMAGES, CORBIS
(AP, BETTMANN), GETTY IMAGES (ADAM BETTCHER,
SCOTT CUNNINGHAM, BRUCE DIERDORFF, STEPHEN
DUNN, NATE FINE/NFL, TOM HAUCK/ALLSPORT, HARRY
HOW, KURT HUTTON/PICTURE POST, GENE LOWER,
G. NEWMAN LOWRANCE, CHRIS MCGRATH, NFL, NFL
PHOTOS, CHRISTIAN PETERSEN, MIKE POWELL,
PRO FOOTBALL HALL OF FAME, GEORGE ROSE, HERB
SCHARFMAN/SPORTS IMAGERY, PAUL SPINELLI,
SPORTING NEWS, JAMIE SQUIRE, BRIAN STABLYK,
KEVIN TERRELL, GREG TROTT, DILIP VISHWANAT,
HERBERT WEITMAN/NFL)

LIBRARY OF CONGRESS CATALOGING-IN-PUBLICATION DATA
WHITING, JIM.
THE STORY OF THE ARIZONA CARDINALS / BY JIM WHITING.
P. CM. — (NFL TODAY)
INCLUDES INDEX.
SUMMARY: THE HISTORY OF THE NATIONAL FOOTBALL
LEAGUE'S ARIZONA CARDINALS, SURVEYING THE
FRANCHISE'S BIGGEST STARS AND MOST MEMORABLE
MOMENTS FROM ITS INAUGURAL SEASON IN 1898 TO
TODAY.
ISBN 978-1-60818-292-3
1. ARIZONA CARDINALS (FOOTBALL TEAM)—HISTORY—
JUVENILE LITERATURE. I. TITLE.

GV956.A75W55 2013
796.332'640979173—DC23   2012027136

FIRST EDITION
9 8 7 6 5 4 3 2 1

COVER: WIDE RECEIVER LARRY FITZGERALD
PAGE 2: RUNNING BACK CHRIS WELLS
PAGES 4-5: UNIVERSITY OF PHOENIX STADIUM
PAGE 6: DEFENSIVE BACK RALPH BROWN

TABLE OF CONTENTS

SIDELINE STORIES

MEET THE CARDINALS

PHOENIX EMERGED IN THE SCORCHING HEAT OF A DESERT VALLEY

A Windy City Start

Few people outside Arizona have heard of the Hohokam Indian tribe. Aided by a complex irrigation system, the Hohokams established a village later called Pueblo Grande in the American Southwest that endured for centuries before being abandoned in the 1400s. When settlers arrived some 400 years later and established a town, they named it Phoenix after the mythical bird that rises from ashes to begin life anew. In 1889, the town became the capital of the Arizona Territory; it maintained that status when Arizona became a state in 1912.

Phoenix's growth was relatively slow. By 1950, it had a population of just over 100,000, ranking 99th among American cities. Then the advent of inexpensive air conditioning in the 1950s ushered in a period of explosive growth. Phoenix's burgeoning size made it attractive to professional sports franchises. The city acquired its first pro team, the Phoenix Suns of the National Basketball Association, in 1968. Three decades later, the creation of the Arizona Diamondbacks Major League Baseball team made

THE CARDINALS FRANCHISE HAS ITS ROOTS IN THE MUDDY TURF OF CHICAGO

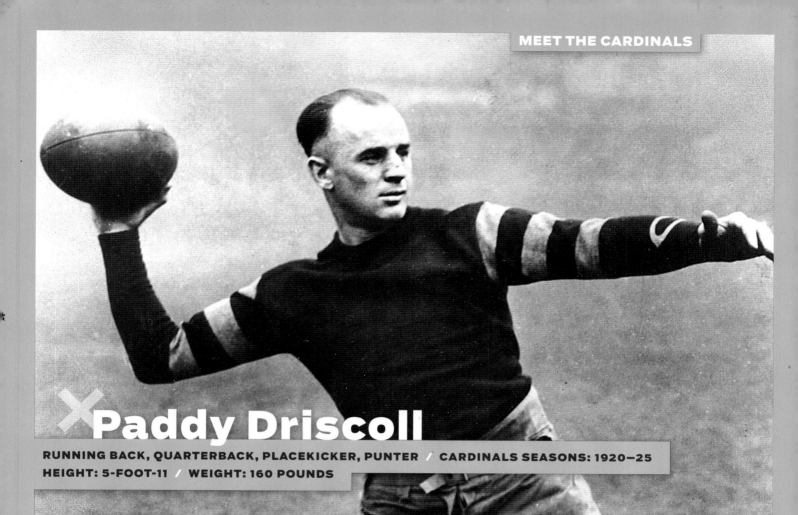

Paddy Driscoll

RUNNING BACK, QUARTERBACK, PLACEKICKER, PUNTER / **CARDINALS SEASONS: 1920–25**
HEIGHT: 5-FOOT-11 / **WEIGHT: 160 POUNDS**

It might not seem like much by today's standards, but the $300 John "Paddy" Driscoll was paid for each game he played for the Cardinals in the 1920s was a huge sum then. But Driscoll was worth it. He was an exceptional quarterback who could also run the ball and even play defense. His real skill, however, came from his kicking leg. Driscoll drop-kicked field goals with remarkable accuracy and sent punts amazing distances. In one game in 1925, he booted four field goals. On more than one occasion, he was responsible for all the Cardinals' points scored in a game: in one 1923 game, he singlehandedly scored 27 points. Driscoll was especially effective against the Chicago Cardinals' crosstown rivals, the Bears. In 1922, he scored all the points accumulated in both matchups between the two teams—six in one game and nine in the other. That made it all the more painful to fans when, in 1926, the Cardinals traded him to the Bears. Driscoll played four more seasons in Chicago before retiring in 1929.

THE CHICAGO CARDINALS WORE PLAIN WHITE HELMETS UNTIL THEY MOVED TO ST. LOUIS

Phoenix just the 10th United States city with franchises in all four major pro sports (with the National Hockey League's Phoenix Coyotes having appeared in 1996). Sandwiched between the Suns and Diamondbacks was the 1988 arrival of the Arizona Cardinals of the National Football League (NFL), a club with a history that stretched back 90 years.

The Cardinals started out far from Arizona. In 1898, a house painter named Chris O'Brien organized a football team on the south side of Chicago, Illinois, called the Morgan Athletic Club. It moved to Normal Field on Racine Avenue a year later and became the Racine Normals. In 1901, O'Brien bought a set of castoff maroon jerseys from the University of Chicago. "That's not maroon. It's cardinal red!" O'Brien said, referring to the color of the robes worn by cardinals—high-ranking officials—of the Catholic Church. The team was renamed the Cardinals (though the cardinal bird wouldn't become part of the club's official logo until 1947).

Finding competition was tough, so the Racine Cardinals disbanded in 1906. O'Brien reestablished the team seven years later, only to soon run up against World War I (when the U.S. joined the fray in 1917) and the worldwide flu pandemic (in 1918). Again the Cardinals suspended operations.

"That's not maroon. It's cardinal red!"

CHRIS O'BRIEN

he third time was the charm for the Cardinals. In 1920, O'Brien plunked down $100 to join the new American Professional Football Association (APFA). The franchise would never go out of operation again. To boost attendance and compete with the crosstown rival Chicago Tigers, O'Brien signed star halfback and quarterback John "Paddy" Driscoll, one of the first superstars in pro football. The Tigers folded after one year, but a new rival arose almost immediately as the Decatur Staleys moved to "The Windy City" in 1921. The following year saw a bevy of name changes. The APFA became the NFL. The Chicago Staleys became the Chicago Bears. And with a team from Racine, Wisconsin, entering the league, O'Brien changed his franchise's name to the Chicago Cardinals.

From 1922 to 1925, the Cardinals split six games with the Bears, plus one tie. In 1925, the Cardinals' 11–2–1 record was the best in the league, earning them the NFL championship. The Bears, though, were winning the battle for fans. With attendance dwindling, O'Brien sold the team to Chicago doctor David Jones in 1929. Jones's first move was coaxing 26-year-old Ernie Nevers—a star for the Duluth Eskimos as a fullback, kicker, punter, and linebacker—out of early retirement. Nevers was an outstanding athlete who had played three pro sports in 1927: football, baseball (as a pitcher, he gave up two home runs to Babe Ruth), and basketball. Although Nevers sparked the team to a decisive victory over the Bears in his first season, the Cardinals finished 6–6–1 that year. With Nevers as coach, the team went a middling 10–10–2 the next two seasons combined. In 1932, Nevers retired.

Nevers's departure coincided with the arrival of new owner Charles Bidwill. By 1935, Bidwill's Cardinals had improved to 6–4–2. Unfortunately, the team couldn't keep the momentum going. Bringing Nevers back to coach the team in 1939 didn't help. The Cardinals managed only one win that year.

World War II slammed the Cardinals, as many players left football behind for military service. In 1943 and 1944, the Cardinals posted a combined 0–20 record. Then, on October 14, 1945, rookie quarterback Paul Christman led the Cardinals to a stunning 16–7 upset victory over the Bears. Although that was the team's only win in 1945, it snapped a 29-game losing streak and established Christman as the Cardinals' quarterback of the future.

A Controversial Championship

In the NFL's early days, season records determined league champions. When the Pottsville (Pennsylvania) Maroons beat the Cardinals 21–7 on December 6, 1925, they believed their 10–2 record gave them the title over the 9–2–1 Chicago. Before their final game, the Maroons played an exhibition game that league president Joseph Carr didn't authorize. Carr suspended the Maroons, ending their season. Cardinals owner Chris O'Brien promptly scheduled games against two of the league's worst teams (one was so short-handed it used several high school players) and easily won both to finish 11–2–1. When the owners met after the season, they awarded the championship to the Cardinals. O'Brien turned it down. He said he scheduled the final two games only as a way of persuading the crosstown Bears to play his team again, adding that the Maroons had beaten his team on the field. The Cardinals accepted the title when the Bidwills became owners in 1932, but Pottsville fans still protest. The NFL took up the issue twice, each time voting to let the Cardinals keep the title. Pittsburgh Steelers owner Dan Rooney objected. "What's been done to this town [Pottsville] and this team—it's not right," he said. "It needs to be fixed."

THE 1925 CARDINALS—MAROONS CONTROVERSY REMAINS AN ONGOING TOPIC

Charles W. Bidwill Sr.

TEAM OWNER / CARDINALS SEASONS: 1933—47

Charles Bidwill (pictured, right) loved football. He had been a vice president of the Chicago Bears before an opportunity came up that he couldn't refuse: owning a professional football franchise, even if it was his team's crosstown rival. Bidwill left the Bears and their winning ways to buy the struggling Cardinals for $50,000 in 1932. Although that losing trend continued for most of his tenure as owner, Bidwill never lost hope or gave up on his team. But like any good businessman, Bidwill wanted to see a return on his investment. So, in 1946, he entered a bidding war against the New York Yankees football team (a franchise in a competing pro league) to sign Charley Trippi (pictured, left), a high-stepping, fast-as-lightning halfback from the University of Georgia. After the Yankees maxed out their offer at $75,000, Bidwill presented a $100,000, 4-year deal to Trippi, believing that Trippi would lead the Cardinals to a championship. He was right, but he didn't live long enough to see it. In April 1947, Bidwill died at the age of 51. His team won the NFL championship just eight months later.

Pro Football's Oldest Record

Star fullback Ernie Nevers turned the much-anticipated matchup between the Cardinals and the Bears on Thanksgiving Day, 1929, into a one-man show. It was a cold, soggy day at Comiskey Park, so Cardinals coach Dewey Scanlon went to basic football. He told Nevers "to blast away at the Bears' middle linemen." Nevers did. He scored twice in the first quarter on runs of 20 and 5 yards, then added a third touchdown on a 6-yard plunge in the second quarter. He also kicked two extra points as the Cardinals took a 20–0 halftime lead. After a third-quarter Bears score, the Cardinals marched back down the field. Nevers scored his fourth touchdown from one yard out and booted the extra point. He added two more touchdowns on short runs in the final period and a fourth extra point before coming out of the game to a standing ovation with five minutes left. Legendary Bears coach George Halas grumbled, "The final score: Bears 6, Nevers 40." He had scored every Cardinals point in a 40–6 victory, setting a single-game record that remains the NFL's oldest unbroken mark. In later years, the humble Nevers deflected attention to his teammates, saying, "But what about the horses up front? They made it all possible."

ERNIE NEVERS WAS ONCE CALLED "THE FOOTBALL PLAYER WITHOUT A FAULT"

THE 1947 CHAMPIONSHIP SQUAD WAS ANCHORED BY YOUNG MEN FRESH FROM WAR

L—R: ELMER ANGSMAN (#7), JIMMY CONZELMAN, AND CHARLEY TRIPPI

Championship Cards

Cardinals coach Jimmy Conzelman soon converted Chicago's offense to a T-formation built around the strong-armed Christman. Churning fullback Pat Harder lined up directly behind Christman, flanked by halfbacks Elmer Angsman and Marshall Goldberg. In 1946, that combination led the Cardinals to a 6–5 record, including a glorious 35–28 victory over the Bears in the final game to end 10 years of non-winning seasons.

That promising finish inspired Bidwill to invest more money. Before the 1947 season, he signed Charley Trippi—a sensational running back from the University of Georgia—to a contract worth $100,000. The amount was a small fortune in those days, but Trippi was worth it to the Cardinals.

The "Dream Backfield" of Christman, Harder, Angsman, and Trippi led the Cardinals to a 9–3 record in 1947. In the final game of the season, the "Cards" met the Bears in a battle for the Western Division title. The Cardinals opened the game with an 80-

CHARLEY TRIPPI (RIGHT) WAS CELEBRATED AS AN ALL-AMERICAN GRIDIRON HERO

19

Ollie Matson

RUNNING BACK / CARDINALS SEASONS: 1952, 1954—58 / HEIGHT: 6-FOOT-2 / WEIGHT: 220 POUNDS

Ollie Matson was the Cardinals' first-round pick in the 1952 NFL Draft. But the fleet-footed star from the University of San Francisco couldn't sign his contract immediately. First, Matson wanted to run as a member of the U.S. track team in the 1952 Summer Olympics in Helsinki, Finland. He won a bronze medal in the 400-meter race and a silver medal in the 1,600-meter relay, then brought his world-class speed to Chicago. As a rookie, Matson earned both Pro Bowl and All-Pro honors. He trained on sandy beaches during the off-season to challenge himself and pick up more speed each year. In his 5 years with the Cardinals, he totaled 3,331 rushing yards and 40 touchdowns. "I'm disappointed if I don't make a long run in a game because I know people come and pay their good money to see me make long runs," Matson once said. "I like to please them." So large was Matson's role in the offense that when the Cardinals traded him to the Los Angeles Rams in 1958, they received nine players in return. In 1972, Matson was inducted into the Pro Football Hall of Fame.

yard touchdown pass, then intercepted four Bears passes. Their 30–21 victory earned them the division crown and a matchup with the Philadelphia Eagles for the league championship.

That game, played on a frozen field at Chicago's Comiskey Park, was bittersweet. The Cardinals won 28–21, thanks to scoring runs by Trippi and Angsman and a fourth-quarter interception by Goldberg. But Bidwill was not around to see it happen. He died before the season started, leaving the team in the hands of his wife, Violet.

The Cardinals enjoyed another outstanding season in 1948, compiling an 11–1 record that still stands as the best in franchise history. Chicago again took on Philadelphia in the title game. With a blizzard blanketing Philadelphia's Shibe Park, the Eagles scored the only touchdown of the game and won 7–0. Coach Conzelman retired after the season, exhausted by the challenges of keeping the Cardinals competitive. "It's a rough business, this winning," he said.

A 6–5–1 season in 1949 was the Cardinals' last winning effort for several years. Even with speedy running back Ollie Matson and punishing defensive back Dick "Night Train" Lane, the Cardinals would tally a miserable 33–84 record throughout the 1950s. As the last game of the 1953 season approached, the Cardinals were still winless for the year. A desperate coach Joe Stydahar threatened to withhold his players' paychecks if they lost. The motivated Cardinals rallied to win that game, 24–17, ending the season 1–10–1.

Wartime Measures

When the U.S. entered World War II in 1941, thousands of American men dutifully reported for service. Almost 1,000 of them were players, coaches, or managers from the NFL, including more than a dozen from the Chicago Cardinals. Offensive end Keith Birlem, defensive end Chuck Braidwood, halfback Chet Wetterlund, and coach Jack Chevigny were among the 23 men from the NFL who were killed in action. While they were fighting in Europe and the South Pacific, their teammates back in Chicago tried to field a team. It became so difficult to keep enough men in the lineup that, in 1944, the Cardinals combined forces with the Pittsburgh Steelers and played as the Card-Pitts. The team was co-coached by Chicago's Phil Handler and Pittsburgh's Walt Kiesling, who had once played for the Cardinals. Only 7,000 fans showed up when the team, which split its home schedule between Comiskey Park in Chicago and Forbes Field in Pittsburgh, played in Chicago. The Card-Pitts didn't win any games that season, leading some frustrated fans to mockingly call the 0–12 club the "Carpets" for the way opponents walked all over them.

FOOTBALL WAS GREATLY DIMINISHED IN IMPORTANCE BY WAR IN THE 1940s

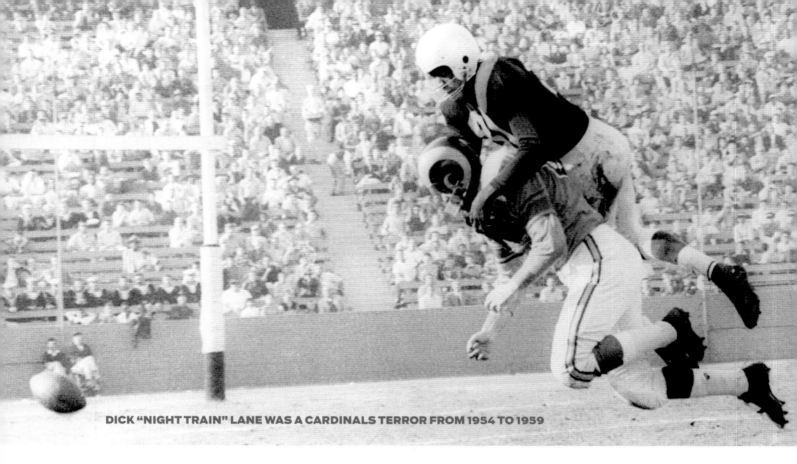

DICK "NIGHT TRAIN" LANE WAS A CARDINALS TERROR FROM 1954 TO 1959

By 1959, things had gotten ugly in Chicago. While the Bears enjoyed successful seasons and a packed stadium, the Cardinals were losing both games and fans. Matson was traded as the team lost 10 of 12 games that year. Revenue plunged, making it clear that Chicago couldn't continue to support two teams. In 1960, the Bidwill family announced that the Cardinals would move to St. Louis, Missouri, where another Cardinals team was already playing baseball.

The change of scenery helped the Cardinals. In 1960, running back John David Crow set a team single-season rushing record with 1,071 yards, and wide receiver Sonny Randle led the league with 15 touchdowns. The team, which shared Sportsman's Park with the baseball-playing Cardinals, won just six games but gained thousands of new fans.

Aside from a woeful 1962 season in which owner Violet Bidwill died and the Cardinals went 4–9–1, the team settled into a winning groove that lasted for most of the decade. Tight end Jackie Smith helped key the offense, while the defense was anchored by safety Larry Wilson, whose intensity impressed both teammates and opponents. Former New York Giants coach Allie Sherman once called Wilson "the goingest player I ever saw."

Despite their improved play, the Cardinals' playoff drought continued. Then, in 1966, the Cardinals signed undrafted quarterback Jim Hart. Hart, who would play 18 seasons and set most of the team's

CHARLEY JOHNSON (PICTURED) MANNED THE QUARTERBACK SPOT BEFORE JIM HART

passing records, was soon joined by speedy wide receiver Mel Gray, halfback Terry Metcalf, and an offensive line led by mountainous tackle Dan Dierdorf. Although the Cardinals remained outside the playoffs for the rest of the decade, they became an exciting team to watch. The club developed such a knack for come-from-behind victories (and suffered more than a few frustrating near misses along the way) in the late 1960s and early '70s that the media began calling it the "Cardiac Cardinals."

The heart-pumping action culminated in 1974, when the Cardinals won their first seven games and finished the season 10–4, good enough to win the National Football Conference (NFC) East Division championship. For the first time in 26 years, they were in the postseason. The Minnesota Vikings defeated the Cardinals in the first round of the 1974 playoffs, but players and fans believed the franchise had turned the corner.

Bought by the Bidwills

The Bidwill family has owned the Cardinals for more than 80 years. That stretch of continuous ownership began in 1932, when Charles W. Bidwill Sr., a vice president of the Chicago Bears, decided to buy his team's fiercest competitors, the Chicago Cardinals. Bidwill was willing to spend money to turn the team into a champion, which eventually happened in 1947. By then, however, Bidwill had passed away and left the team to his wife, Violet. All that time, their two boys, William ("Bill") and Charles Jr., had been sitting through practices and serving as ball boys during games. So when Mrs. Bidwill, the first female owner in the NFL, died just two years after managing the team's move from Chicago to St. Louis in 1960, it was only natural that she would leave the team to her sons. In 1972, Bill and his family became sole owners of the team, while Charles became managing general partner. In 1996, another generation got involved as Bill's son Michael (pictured) joined the organization and eventually became the team's president.

MICHAEL BIDWILL CARRIED ON A THREE-GENERATION FAMILY TRADITION IN ARIZONA

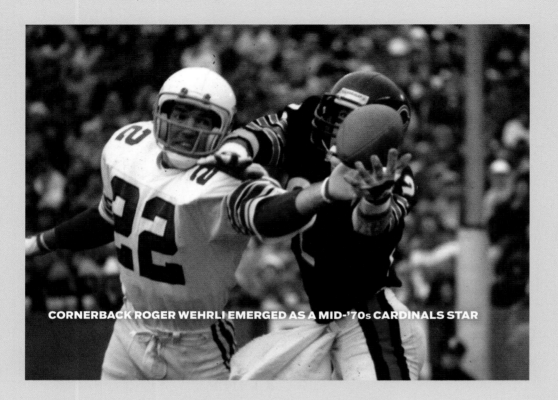

CORNERBACK ROGER WEHRLI EMERGED AS A MID-'70s CARDINALS STAR

Hello, Arizona

When the Cardinals won the division again in 1975, fans really began to believe, even though St. Louis lost 35–23 in the playoffs to the Los Angeles Rams. The 1976 season started well, with the Cards reaching midseason at 5–2. Then a controversial missed pass interference call in a Thanksgiving Day game against the Dallas Cowboys led to a loss that eventually bumped the 10–4 team out of playoff contention. "It's a shame," general manager Joe Sullivan said as the season ended. "This is the best team we've had."

By the end of 1977, however, that team was falling apart. St. Louis couldn't manage a winning record, much less a playoff berth, until the strike-shortened 1982 season, when the 5–4 Cardinals were among 16 teams invited to a special Super Bowl tournament. In the first game, the Cardinals fell 41–16 to the Green Bay Packers.

In 1983, with young quarterback Neil Lomax connecting with All-Pro wide receiver Roy Green for 1,227 yards and a league-leading 14 touchdowns, the Cardinals put together an

JIM HART'S PASSING HELPED CARRY THE CARDINALS TO THE PLAYOFFS THREE TIMES

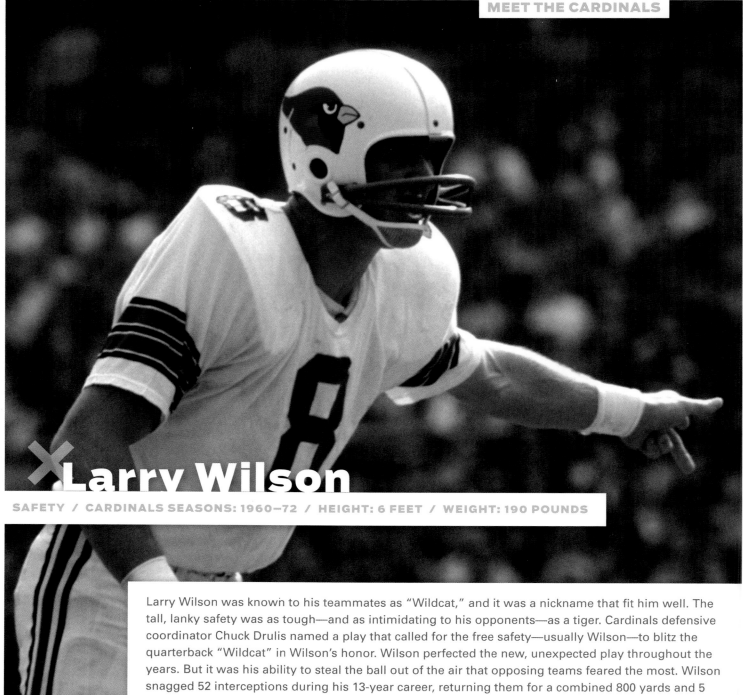

Larry Wilson

SAFETY / CARDINALS SEASONS: 1960–72 / HEIGHT: 6 FEET / WEIGHT: 190 POUNDS

Larry Wilson was known to his teammates as "Wildcat," and it was a nickname that fit him well. The tall, lanky safety was as tough—and as intimidating to his opponents—as a tiger. Cardinals defensive coordinator Chuck Drulis named a play that called for the free safety—usually Wilson—to blitz the quarterback "Wildcat" in Wilson's honor. Wilson perfected the new, unexpected play throughout the years. But it was his ability to steal the ball out of the air that opposing teams feared the most. Wilson snagged 52 interceptions during his 13-year career, returning them for a combined 800 yards and 5 touchdowns. In one 1965 game, with both wrists broken and covered in casts, he intercepted a pass—a demonstration of toughness and determination that coaches have used to motivate ailing players ever since. Wilson ended his playing days in 1972, but he returned to the Cardinals the next year as a scout; in the years that followed, he worked his way up to team vice president. After 43 total years with the Cardinals, Wilson—who was voted into the Hall of Fame in 1978—retired in 2002.

ROY GREEN'S 1,555 RECEIVING YARDS WERE TOPS IN THE NFL IN 1984

improved 8–7–1 record. But neither that nor the team's 9–7 record in 1984 could get St. Louis back to the postseason. Injuries to Lomax, Green, and running back Ottis Anderson stalled the Cards in 1985.

Like their Chicago predecessors, St. Louis fans seemed unwilling to suffer through any more losses. By 1987, team owner William "Bill" Bidwill, Charles Bidwill's son, was frustrated by the city's refusal to replace Busch Stadium, which held fewer fans than all but one other stadium in the NFL. He started looking for sunnier skies under which to play.

Bidwill found those sunny skies in Phoenix, Arizona. The Phoenix Cardinals' new home, Sun Devil Stadium on the campus of Arizona State University (located in nearby Tempe), was full for the team's first home game, a 17–14 loss to the Cowboys on September 12, 1988. Lomax, Green, and explosive wide receiver J. T. Smith gave the new fan base something to cheer about, as Lomax threw for nearly 3,400 yards on the year. Although the 1988 season ended with 5 consecutive losses and a 7–9 record, the team set a single-season record for attendance at 472,937. Arizona seemed like a happy home.

However, Lomax's happiness didn't last long. An arthritic hip forced the 30-year-old quarterback to retire before the start of the 1990 campaign. Then Green was traded after the team suffered through a miserable season. With veteran leadership in short supply, the Cardinals lost the last eight games of the 1991 season to finish 4–12, a record they duplicated in 1992.

The team's rebuilding efforts, including the drafting of running back Garrison Hearst in 1993 and the hiring of defensive mastermind Buddy Ryan as head coach in 1994, helped the Cardinals climb out of the NFC East cellar. Now known as the Arizona Cardinals, the team improved to 8–8 in 1994. But as Hearst recovered from a knee injury and Ryan's motivational tactics failed,

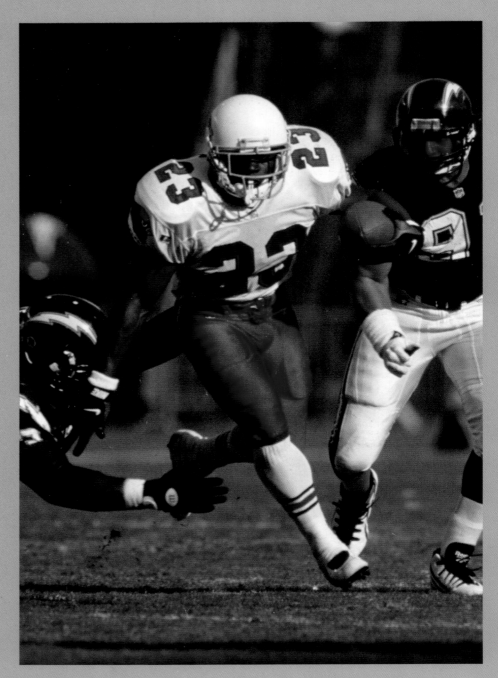

Home Sweet Home

There wasn't much excitement for the Arizona Cardinals or their fans in 2000, when the team lost all but three of its games. But the Cardinals scored a major victory that year when the citizens of Maricopa County, where the franchise is based, voted to help fund a new stadium for the team. The Cardinals, who had never played in a park of their own design, took the opportunity to dream big about what it would include—and most of their wishes came true. When the finished product was unveiled six years later, the University of Phoenix Stadium had both a retractable roof and a retractable natural grass field that could move outside the stadium's walls to flourish in the sun when the team was not playing. Perhaps more importantly, the stadium had additional seating, which the owners hoped would translate into additional revenue and, in turn, a more competitive team. "There is a direct correlation between revenue from new stadiums and being able to compete," said team president Michael Bidwill. "The teams with new stadiums are consistently in the playoffs." Since moving into their new home, the Cardinals have earned two playoff berths and a trip to the Super Bowl.

THE UNIVERSITY OF PHOENIX STADIUM WAS BUILT AT A COST OF $455 MILLION

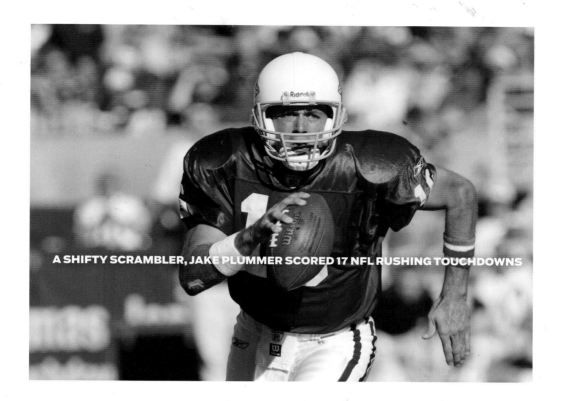

A SHIFTY SCRAMBLER, JAKE PLUMMER SCORED 17 NFL RUSHING TOUCHDOWNS

Arizona seemed to wilt again, falling back to the bottom of the standings in 1995.

The 1996 season started with a new coach, Vince Tobin, and a new quarterback, Boomer Esiason. Although Esiason, who had led the Cincinnati Bengals to the Super Bowl a decade earlier, was nearing the end of his career, he led Arizona on a 3-game winning streak that included a 522-yard passing performance (third-best in NFL history) against the Washington Redskins as the Cardinals finished the season a respectable 7–9.

With Esiason contemplating retirement in the off-season, Tobin knew the offense needed a spark. In the 1997 NFL Draft, the Cardinals thought they had acquired that spark in Arizona State University quarterback Jake Plummer. Known as Jake "The Snake" for his ability to slip away from defenders, Plummer had led the Sun Devils to an undefeated season in 1996 and a berth in the Rose Bowl. In 1998, Plummer led the Cardinals to a 9–7 record and their first playoff appearance in 16 years.

Behind solid efforts from Plummer and running back Adrian Murrell, Arizona took a 20–0 lead against the Cowboys and won 20–7 for its first postseason victory in 51 years. Finally, the Cardinals had something to celebrate. "The past is the past," Plummer said. "You live in the present. Now, we are ready to go into the future." The future was short-lived, though, as the Cardinals lost to the Vikings a week later. Still, for the time being, hope had been restored.

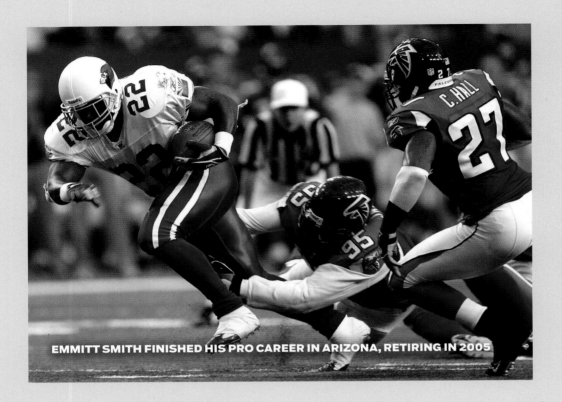

EMMITT SMITH FINISHED HIS PRO CAREER IN ARIZONA, RETIRING IN 2005

A New Century

Unfortunately, that sense of hope quickly evaporated as the Cardinals returned to their losing ways. In the middle of the 2000 season, Coach Tobin was dismissed, and the Cardinals tumbled to last place in the NFC East with a 3–13 mark. Plummer's star, too, had fallen. In 1999, the gunslinging quarterback threw 24 interceptions and only 9 touchdown passes. In 2002, after Arizona's second last-place finish in three years, he left town to play for the Denver Broncos.

In 2003, the Cardinals made headlines by signing former Cowboys running back Emmitt Smith, who was the all-time league leader in career rushing yards and touchdowns. Although Smith was 34 years old, the Cardinals believed the future Hall-of-Famer still had some great performances in him. With promising young receiver Anquan Boldin also added to the lineup, Arizona expected a marked improvement. Boldin had an immediate impact in 2003, tallying the most receptions (101) by a rookie receiver in NFL history. But Smith was sidelined with a shoulder injury, and the Cardinals went just 4–12.

ANQUAN BOLDIN WAS KNOWN AS ONE OF THE STRONGEST RECEIVERS IN FOOTBALL

✕Jackie Smith

TIGHT END / CARDINALS SEASONS: 1963–77 / HEIGHT: 6-FOOT-4 / WEIGHT: 235 POUNDS

Jackie Smith had good hands. The Cardinals relied on those hands to haul in receptions and on his fast feet (Smith was also a track standout in college) to reach the end zone once he made the catch. Smith, who played all but the final year of his NFL career with the Cardinals, finished his career with 480 receptions for a total of 7,918 yards (the most by a tight end in the NFL until 1990) and 43 touchdowns. But he was such a versatile athlete that he was also handed the Cardinals' punting duties during his first three seasons. Although he was a pivotal player in the Cardinals' two playoff appearances in the 1970s (1974 and 1975), it is his postseason play with Dallas that most fans remember. In 1978, Smith signed with the Super Bowl–bound Cowboys. He dropped a third-down pass late in the Super Bowl, forcing the Cowboys to kick a field goal. When Dallas lost by four points, Smith became the scapegoat. He retired from football before the next season started and was inducted into the Hall of Fame in 1994.

As construction began on a new Cardinals stadium in Glendale, just west of Phoenix, the team hired the 33rd coach in its history. That coach was Dennis Green, who had previously led the Vikings to the playoffs 8 times in 10 years. "I'm here for one reason," Green said as the season started. "Because I believe with all my heart that we can build ourselves an outstanding program."

Green began building by drafting wide receiver Larry Fitzgerald, who had nearly won the Heisman Trophy (given to college football's best player) as a sophomore at the University of Pittsburgh, as the third overall pick of the 2004 NFL Draft. But no matter how much Green believed, Arizona wasn't ready to be a champion. That year, the

MATT LEINART WAS UNABLE TO FIND THE STARDOM THAT MANY HAD PREDICTED

team mourned the loss of former safety Pat Tillman—who had quit football to join the U.S. Army and was subsequently killed in Afghanistan—but couldn't even win the game at which they honored the fallen hero. The Cardinals finished 6–10.

In 2005, the Cardinals brought in two-time NFL Most Valuable Player (MVP) Kurt Warner, a former Rams quarterback. But neither he nor newly acquired running back Edgerrin James could get the Cardinals above the .500 mark. Even moving into the luxurious new University of Phoenix Stadium in 2006 wasn't enough. By the end of a 5–11 season in 2006, Coach Green had lost both his patience and his job.

With new coach Ken Whisenhunt at the helm and rookie quarterback Matt Leinart leading the offense, the Cardinals rebounded to win eight games and finish second in the NFC West Division in 2007. Then, in 2008, Arizona really soared. The veteran Warner was named the team's starting quarterback and rediscovered his old MVP form. As he slung the ball to Boldin, Fitzgerald, and Steve Breaston—who became just the fifth trio of receivers ever to each post more than 1,000 receiving yards in a season—the Cardinals opened with 7 wins in their first 10 games. Although they won just two more games, their 9–7 record was good enough to win their division and return to the playoffs. Few experts saw them as a serious contender, but Arizona defied the odds, beating three opponents—the Atlanta Falcons, Carolina Panthers, and Philadelphia Eagles—to reach its first Super Bowl.

Keeping the Lid On

Super Bowl XLIII, played after the 2008 season, marked Arizona's first appearance on football's grandest stage. The game also marked the first time in NFL history that a sportswriter father covered his player son in the big game. Larry Fitzgerald Sr.—the father of the Cardinals' standout wide receiver—was a longtime columnist for the *Minnesota Spokesman-Recorder* and had reported on the Super Bowl for many years. Larry Sr. was fully aware of the long-established media practice that prohibits sportswriters from cheering while attending games. "I'm there as an objective journalist," he said. "On the outside, that's what you see. But inside, I'm high-fiving." The proud father must have done a lot of inside high-fiving during the Super Bowl, as his son snagged 7 passes for 127 yards and 2 scores. The second touchdown covered 64 yards with 2:37 remaining and gave the Cardinals a 27–23 lead, though Pittsburgh came back to score two minutes later and win the game. When the game was over and father and son got together, the emotion really came out. "Later, when we watch the [tape of the game], I'm able to jump up and down and yell," Larry Sr. said. "I'm happy for him. I am his father."

LARRY FITZGERALD EARNED A REPUTATION AS ARGUABLY FOOTBALL'S PREMIER WIDEOUT

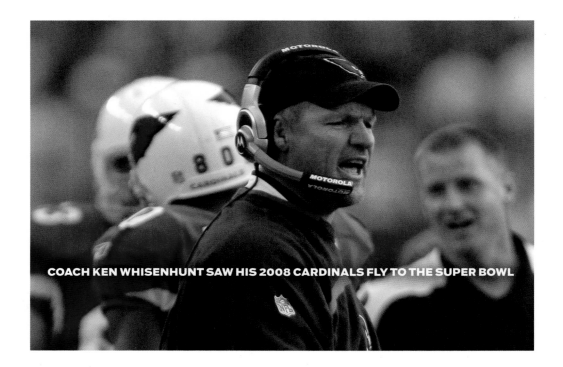

COACH KEN WHISENHUNT SAW HIS 2008 CARDINALS FLY TO THE SUPER BOWL

uper Bowl XLIII pitted the Cardinals against the Steelers, who featured the NFL's top-ranked defense. Arizona started slowly and trailed 20–7 in the third quarter. But behind Warner, who passed for 377 yards, and defensive tackle Darnell Dockett, the Cardinals staged a furious comeback, seizing a 23–20 lead on a 64-yard scoring strike to Fitzgerald late in the fourth quarter. The Steelers, though, marched down the field to score the winning touchdown with just 35 seconds remaining. It was a heartbreaking loss, but what a ride it had been. "I am so proud of this football team," Warner said. "We gave ourselves a chance to win a world championship, but that other team went out and won it."

The Cardinals continued to roll in 2009, going 10–6 to repeat as division champions. It marked the first time the franchise had won that many regular-season games in 33 years. In the first round of the playoffs, the Cardinals opened up a 17–0 first-quarter lead against the visiting Green Bay Packers. The Packers stormed back to tie the game 45–45 and force overtime. But Cardinals linebacker Karlos Dansby rumbled 17 yards with a recovered fumble to give Arizona a 51–45 win, with the two teams' combined 96 points setting an NFL postseason scoring record. The next week, though, the eventual Super Bowl champion New Orleans Saints thumped the Cardinals 45–14. Warner announced his retirement soon afterward.

The Cardinals opened the 2010 season 3–2 but then slid to a 5–11 finish. In the off-season, Arizona filled its quarterback spot by signing free agent Kevin Kolb. The Cards won their 2011 opener and then dropped six in a row before Kolb was injured. Rookie John Skelton filled in admirably for most of the

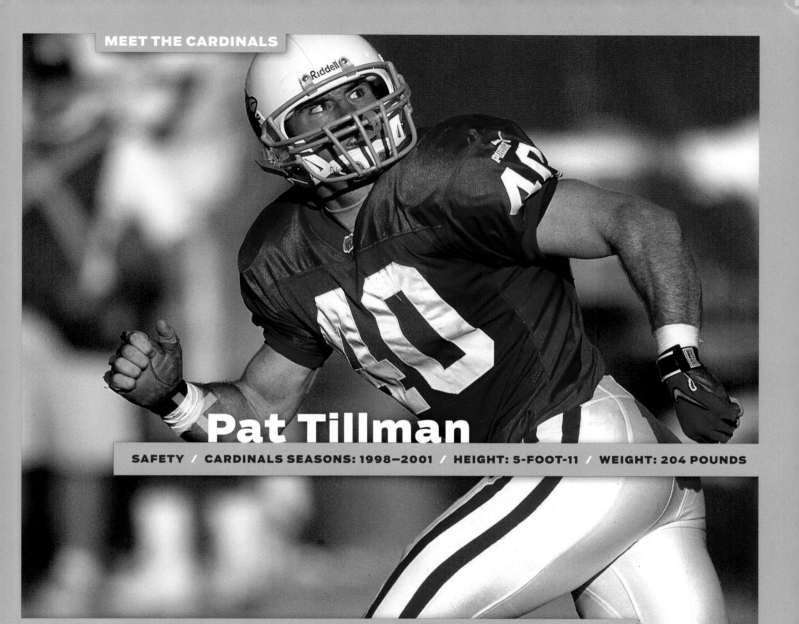

Pat Tillman

SAFETY / CARDINALS SEASONS: 1998–2001 / HEIGHT: 5-FOOT-11 / WEIGHT: 204 POUNDS

In the four short seasons that Pat Tillman played in the NFL, he accumulated 331 tackles, 2.5 sacks, 3 interceptions, and 3 forced fumbles. For a player who was selected with the 226th overall pick in the 1998 NFL Draft, those statistics are impressive. But although many remember his scrappy playing style fondly, Tillman is better known for his decision to enlist, along with his brother Kevin, in the U.S. Army just eight months after the terrorist attacks against America on September 11, 2001. In 2003, he was sent to the Middle East as part of the invasion of Iraq known as Operation Enduring Freedom. He also served in Afghanistan, where, in an accident on April 22, 2004, he was shot and killed by a fellow soldier. On September 19, 2004, every team in the NFL honored Tillman by wearing a memorial sticker on their helmets, and the Cardinals retired jersey number 40 in his honor. "He represented all that was good in sports," Cardinals coach Dave McGinnis said. "He proudly walked away from a career in football to a greater calling."

DARNELL DOCKETT (#90) SWITCHED FROM DEFENSIVE TACKLE TO DEFENSIVE END IN 2009

HARD-HITTING LINEBACKER DARYL WASHINGTON EMERGED AS A BEAST IN 2012

WHEN NOT RETURNING KICKS, PATRICK PETERSON DEALT OUT MANY HARD HITS

rest of the season as the team rallied to finish 8–8. The team's most spectacular rookie, though, was cornerback Patrick Peterson, who returned an NFL record-tying four punts for touchdowns and was the only first-year player selected to the league's 2011 All-Pro team. "He has such a great feel, and he is definitely a force," said Coach Whisenhunt.

The entire Arizona team became a force early in the 2012 season. The Cardinals won their first four games, and some analysts' power rankings put them at the top of the entire NFL. But Arizona won just one additional game for the rest of the season, with the lowlight being a 58–0 drubbing by Seattle. Coach Whisenhunt was then fired. His replacement was Bruce Arians, the interim head coach at Indianapolis, who had taken the 2012 Colts to the playoffs and been named Coach of the Year. Arians had a record of success in developing young quarterbacks such as Ben Roethlisberger and Andrew Luck. Fitzgerald, for one, was in favor of the change. "I have great admiration for my former coaching staff," the wide receiver said. "But I'm excited about our future."

Hopefully this future will justify the faith of the team's followers. Wherever they have played in their long and largely unsuccessful history, the Cardinals have always had a loyal base of fans, even if that base has not always been huge. In 2011, the NFL announced that Arizona would play host to Super Bowl XLIX in 2015. Today's Cardinals hope to give their fans something to shout about by perhaps soon soaring into their home nest at University of Phoenix Stadium for another shot at pro football's biggest prize.